The Motor Hotels of Central Avenue

A Collection of Poetry

PW COVINGTON

Hercules Press

Victoria, TX & Albuquerque, NM

HERCULES PRESS

Back cover author photo - Jason Kurtz
All other photos by author, unless noted
Cover photo: Town Lodge, 4101 Central Ave. NE

1st Edition, November 2017

Foreword by Edward Vidaurre

Hercules Press

Victoria, TX & Albuquerque, NM

THE MOTOR HOTELS OF CENTRAL AVENUE

ISBN: 978-1977886439

Other Books by PW Covington

Poetry:

77901 (*Limited Run, Only available at live readings*) 2016
Sacred Wounds (Slough Press) 2015
I Did Not Go Looking for This 2013

Fiction:

Dear Elsa, Letters from a Texas Prison
2014

Edward Vidaurre, McAllen TX, Nov 2017

PW Covington, Albuquerque NM

Dear PW,

I gave a 27 year-old woman a ride to Pharr, TX today. She was waiting in the rain with her beat toddler in arms. She had a backpack strapped to her back, a large blanket for the child who was already fussy and raining hell in her ears. She looked,

So beat and beautiful,
So blessed, so magic

We were both dropping our kids off at school. So when I asked her if she needed a ride she said yes. When I crossed 10th street I thought of your words,

and what of her?
and what of truth?

Her story: She ran her mother over accidentally, broke every bone in her hand, her husband can't return home to her and the kids until he gets off of drugs. She smiles at me with a suffering search of hope in her eyes. Down to her ocean in hopes. I tell you PW, I admire a good struggle. Your book was a soundtrack this morning. *In Transit* through rain and the Texas humidity, with the ghost bike reminding me of the *Crosses in the Bar Ditch*. A drive to H.E.B. why not?

I have been carrying your manuscript with me everywhere, I spilled coffee on *NOON*, one of my favorite poems in it. I can hear your voice read it to me. Very few have the gift of sounding good live and looking good, on paper. You do both throughout *The Motor Hotels of Central Avenue.* Not from here or there, but from everywhere, plumbing through your travels leaving seeds of poetry as you distance yourself from that cage. You are free, man!

Your book is alive! Depending on where my heart and mind are at the time, there's a poem that speaks to me. And no poems block out other poems, each one is well concocted, which reminds me that we still have to have an absinthe inspired workshop. The green fairy in New Mexico? Last night, at work, all the TV's went awol, messages across all of them. This only happens when the weather is bad. I walked outside and the only thing that stuck was the humidity, there was a stillness, an eeriness to it all. And again I return to a poem, *The Stratosphere Hotel*:

Palms die when they do not learn to sway or swing
And negotiate
Multiple realities of need

Then it fucking rained!

Vicariously through you, I am at Standing Rock through *Shores of the Cannon Ball (Mni Wiconi).* Peering in on the deputies and armed vigilantes. But most importantly, watching the elders and medicine women.

Elders and medicine women dance tonight
Water protectors in small fire lights
Sing songs that never ended
Across the Cannon Ball
Mni Wiconi

It's about so much more than the water
Bit it's about the water first
Mni Wiconi

Your poems put you right there to suffer and fight alongside those going through injustice. I think of the words of Gloria E. Anzaldúa in her poem *The New Speaker,*

"Words are our trade
We speak them soft
We speak them hard...
We are our age's mouthpieces"

I thank you for your poetry. I am happy you're prolific. I love that you travel and fight the good fight. I am honored to be your friend. Now go write that collection of short fiction.

Your brother in poetry,

Vidaurre

Editors Note: Edward Vidaurre is un poeta de la frontera, living in McAllen, Texas.

Check out his latest collection of poetry, "*Chicano Blood Transfusion*" from Flower Song Books, ISBN 978-0692411469

Contents

It is Time to Write a Poem

It is time to write a poem
A poem about riding a Trailways bus through Alabama
A poem about Piggly Wiggly state policemen
And flags and grits
And backyard-bred attack dogs
Gun shows
Southern pride

It is time to write a poem
Because what we've been busy with
    isn't working
These guns and prisons
Banks and borders
These laws and churches
These immigration mazes, religious hatreds
Must all have seemed like good ideas
    at some point

All these wars

When I see your face in the morning
Before the news of day comes charging in
Before the bodies roll in on the digital tide
Before the pragmatism of decades takes hold
It's time to write a poem

It is time to write a poem to mail
    away to foreign lands
To send off to the moon
To the planet Mars
To the core of this Earth
To the cosmic Colorado rubbage man
Because prayer doesn't do the things it used to

It is time to commit poetry

It’s time to write a poem of witness
A Trans Atlantic “YAWP”
A HOWL
A, “Yes, Yes, Y’all…and it don’t stop!”
It is not the time for ballads
I can carry no corrido but my own
It is time to write a poem
    ‘cause it ain’t coming on TV

It’s time to write a poem
Today
On a Tuesday, on a Saturday night
Drunk or sad or covered in sweat
Shivering on a park bench
    or locked away in detention
With tubes and machines hooked to my heart
On our last good day together
Before opening the condom wrapper
Before paying the toll
Before making the reservations
It is time to write a poem

It is time to write a poem
Because we won’t last forever
And no one else is writing about
    the smolder in your eyes
Because all those millennial promises
    never came true
And 17 years is long enough to wait
It is time to write a poem

It is time to write a poem for Highlights magazine
for children in medical waiting rooms
A poem for Sky Mall magazine, glanced at once
    at 30 thousand feet
A poem folded into a box and sold from
    a cigarette vending machine
It is time to write a poem
    use only the sins in your pocket
        use only what you know is yours

Poetry isn’t anything, most days
    but
It is time to write a poem
While we still can

Lazy H Motel, 5601 Central Ave. NE

Texas

Small Schools on County Roads

Small schools on county roads
Glow in the dawn
Sodium vapor and grey overcast
Set the tone

Pickup trucks queue
Billow white fumes
Forty degree morning
Children in camouflage coats
Dash into cafetoriums
To drink whole milk from
Half-pint cartons
They speak of baby Jesus Christmas pageants
White-tailed deer, killed last week

Then it's, "I Pledge Allegiance..."
And, "As we all bow our heads"
Fourth grade structure
Wrapped in
Shelf-stable patriotism
Natural binds of Christian hate

Small schools on county roads
In December
Monkey bars welded from
Surplus oil field pipe

No hope for the future
Small schools on county roads
Stay frozen
    in tradition

Walls

Walls are
The last, futile
Efforts
Of those too timid
Or too weak
To grow wings
And fly

Dustin's Despair

I write a poem to Dustin,
My melancholy Houston friend,
You fall asleep every night
Just down the street from
Rocket ships

Your walls stacked high
With centuries of poetry
Known to you like the curves of a lover
Yet, you torment yourself
With wars toiled on foreign shores
You have never worn a uniform
    and you never will

War is Hellish, brutish, work
I know this
We all know this
But, from time to time
Because man is made of the kind
Of offal that he is
It will always be
Necessary…
War

So; we strive,
Dustin,
To develop
Diversity of character,
To tool and train for war
While schooling and scribing for peace

The Athenian ideal

When I was a boy
My parents took me,
The child of an American airman,
And stood me at that Acropolis
And imagined it, as it was,

When it was first
Conceived and built;
They must have been onto something, Dustin…

That Athenian ideal

It has made it through
All this time…
All these epochs,
Of peace and war
It's outlived all the Gods
And temple whores

Fuck the Spartans, Dustin

You despair too much, Dustin
Even war can hold
Moments of sheer joy
Even love,
Moments of total ruin

And you *have* seen battle, Dustin
We all have
You've been fighting your entire life
Trapped behind the lines that you were born within
You are a warrior of the Athenian ideal
Olympus awaits you,
        off of the Gulf Freeway

To get there, Dustin
We'll have to leave the familiar
Forsake our bookshelves and libraries
Laws and safety,
Learn to fall with no nets
Fly with no parachutes or waxy wings

You despair too much, Dustin
The disaster is waiting
Like it always has
Let's go,

let's go!

And as we tumble through space,
Let us not scream in fear,
Trumpet your mighty and large voice of challenge to heaven, Dustin
Not in despair
But, in joy!

Laundromat Blues

Friday night
7 or so
Washing T-shirts and boxer-briefs
Coin operated
Clink, Clink, Clink

Fat, young mothers
So Beat and beautiful
    they don't even know it
So blessed, so magic
Universal

They tell their only babies
To
"Leave the man alone"
As they scoot on the floor
Before
The Dr. Pepper machine

I am the only man in this place
And so, I must be danger
I must be
Lethal
I must be
Washing the cat pee
    from my yellowing
        white under-shirts
Then,
Into the dryer
Whoosh, Whoosh, Whoosh

I'm sorry, young mothers
For defiling this cleaning place

This sacred space
    with my dirty laundry
        with my searching smile

So, I cross the street
For some Thunderbird wine
And bide my time
Outside
    behind
The Laundromat
Glug, Glug, Glug

Removing stains is never easy
I thought I saw
Herbert Huncke's reflection
Behind the big, silver, clothes dryer
In sheet metal sheen
But,
    it was only me
And angelic Beat toddlers
And coin operated redemption
And cheap, white wine

Pioneer Motel, 7600 Central Avenue SE

Amazon

The UPS delivery driver
Greets me on my front porch
It is the 3rd time we have spoken
This new-born year

"More books," he says
And he bends to
Pet the head
Of my ever-present bulldog

"You must read a lot," he says
"I read more than I write,"
    says I
On this warm, grey
January day

"You make much money
    from all that poetry and writing?"
He asks

My wooden porch, in need of painting

"Just enough," I say,
"To keep you coming here
To drop off boxes."
"Enough, I say,
For you to know my bulldog's name,
    and to know how he likes to be scratched
    behind his right ear."

"Yes," he smiles, and says,
As he walks back to his brown delivery truck;

“We all work for Amazon
These days.”

For the Birds

I hold no deep
Affinity
For the small, brown, birds
That gather
At my red feeder,
Hanging by a wire
From my front yard pecan

But, I spend a portion
Of my Air Force pension
Every week
At the market
To buy packaged seed

I would miss them,
I suppose
If I could not hear
Their peeps and trills

From my sunny, winter, morning
Coffee porch

H.E.B.

Eleven A.M. on a Tuesday
At H.E. B.
The only grocer
In this tiny, Texas, town
    or for 50 miles, around

A half dozen cans of cat food
Pre-packaged deli meat
Three bottles of
The cheapest Chardonnay on the shelf
    and frozen TV-dinners

Six foot four and getting fat
Grateful Dead tie-dye tee
And faded blue jeans
A pledge-drive, NPR, baseball cap,
    grey hair day

Past the Texas magazine rack
Machine guns and serial killers,
No Cosmo nor New Yorker
H.E. B. knows what sells
    down here

The check-out woman,
Her pin says, 20 years of service,
Asks me;

"Do you need help carrying that out,
    Sir?"

Navarro Street

I lost my job at the foundry
Lisa went back down to Tennessee
Winter was coming on
I had no place to be

I had a buddy named Rico, he said
To come on down
He said they're hiring like Hell
In this Eagle Ford town
Meet me in Cuero,
I got a new truck waiting for you

The bottom fell out of oil prices
It was a south Texas oil-bust crisis
I went from cocaine and hookers
To looking for a place to stay
The repo man came
And towed that pickup away

Now, I'm standing out on Navarro Street
Asking strangers for money to get something to eat
It just gets worse,
a little bit every day

Fracking doesn't pay like it used to
The only shoes I own are these steel-toed boots
All I've ever been is an honest, hard-working, man
I'm a little less honest now,
and making it, however I can

I'm on Navarro Street
Holding a sign

And they're cussing at me
Most of the time

"Get a job, go back home, you lazy, white, trash.
Step away from my car,
Stay away from my hard-earned cash."

I should have stayed up in New England
The weather is colder,
But there're temperate seasons,
Even, now and then,
A string of warm, sun-shining days
When a man goes down, up there
He doesn't have to fade away

But, the Eagle Ford was booming
And I needed the change, anyway

I'm out on Navarro
Watching trucks roll by
All I want to do is
Get drunk, or high, or cry
Because the Eagle Ford has crashed
And everything here is gonna die

I notice that you never want to look me
Directly in the eye

From your -350 dually
Jacked up to the sky

Stare too deep, you'll see a little piece of truth;

Ashes to ashes,
When they're finished with you
That pride will be gone,
And what the Hell are you gonna do?

Working Navarro Street,
Living on the sly
Victoria cops don't give a damn or ask why
To be honest, the fuckers don't care if you live or you die
And nobody wants to hear
How hard it is to even try to try

Rico caught a chain from the county jail
He's got 10 years to do, for cooking and sales
When that Eagle Ford drops,
A man does what he's gotta do
Sometimes, out here,
I kind of wish I went with Rico, too

Standing out here on Navarro Street
About the last kind of person you'd ever want to meet
But, don't you worry,
I'll be moving it along some day
But tonight I'm shivering
And looking for a hidden place to lay

The preacher-man's mission won't let me in
I won't kiss his ass,
And I won't say "Amen"
To the things he says I need to believe
If I'm gonna get a bed
Victoria, Texas doesn't want to see ya holdin' up your head

Navarro Street's the kind of place that kills a man
While telling him that he can be whatever he can
As long as you can piss in their cup,
While dancing to their band

No matter what they say
You know what it's all about

The Eagle Ford is over, get your Yankee ass
Headed back out

Climate Change in South Texas

That first
Late
November
Day
You can
Wear
A sweater
Cool
Enough
Now
In Texas
To
Again
Hope
For Changes
In
The new
Year

Noon

Noon
Is a great time
To wake up

Leave the mornings
To car seat Calvinist
Sedans and pick-up trucks

Coming off the
Night watch
The night shift
With pens and scrolls
Star-struck

Moon burned by absinthe
The words we wrote last night
Await the cold
Daylight of
Destruction

Friends made, in the dark
With the dark
Lovers are
Ethereal and gone
Being paid
To stay away

Noon
As the Catholic bells
Of Saint Joseph
Mark the middle
Of carpenter days

Noon time coffee
In Texas solitude
How to get from here
To there?

Poetry is a bridge
Between literature and art

We are crossing
Ourselves
As church bells chime
Twelve times

San Marcos, Texas,
Open Mic

I just, barely, missed the Goddess that night

She stood in the back
The crowded room flowed around her
Like liquid hips
Filling that simple, cotton, dress
An infant in her arms

Bright, beautiful, ocean-filled eyes
Baby child, at ease, among poets
And journals and guitars and
Thom the WorldPoet
Down from Austin for the night

Words and cider and espresso drinks

There were copies of poetry journals
Little magazines
The Mas Tequila Review
Harbinger Asylum
Self-published chapbooks

Desperate missives
From land-locked poets
Half-cocked

Central Texas
Sweet Spot
Hot

Hanging on to the edges
Of a room packed with undergrads

Fringe-livers, Side-liners
Midnight drivers

Ambivalent Anarchists; mostly

My eyes would not peel away from her
Child-bearing shoulders
She is goddess and whore
Madonna with child
Everything I've ever wanted
Everything I could never keep
Poetry in skin tones

Life bearing,
Soul sharing,
Flesh

Dancing somewhere,
In tidal pools
Under a full-moon glow

With never a need for a stage
Or microphone

The room swirls, on Ganja smoke
And the word-mother with child is gone,
Leaving only little magazines
That no one reads,
Behind

Poetry will attract,

Yet rarely; rarely, can it capture

I just, barely, missed the goddess that night

Crosses in the Bar Ditch

All over Texas
You can see them
If you look

More and more of them, as you head south
The crosses in the bar ditches
Whisper
They can be hard to hear
Through the oil field drone
Over angry, country, radio

But, they are there
To remind
To warn
To witness
All of the dreams that never arrived
At the places they were hoping for…

Bluebonnets sprout from salty tears
Until neglect and cactus
And brutal summer comes

Slow down

And listen

To the empty prayers
The cries for mercy
Unrequited,
To the crosses in the bar ditch

San Antonio, Mixed and Matched

I cut up my Sunday Express News
To take a look at the places between spaces
Looking for light
Worlds between worlds y palabras in the margins
Viva Tacoland and Uncle Sam
San Fernando cemeteries
The Mission Drive-In and puffy tacos
Barbacoa and Bill Miller, everywhere
Big Red stains on gringo lips
Cut up city; mixed and matched
Like cascarone confetti

The Ponderosa, 10600 Central Ave. SE

In Transit

Motion
Wheels and air brakes
Traffic lights and handshakes
Face down in Facebook
Smart phone, Smart ass
Sideways looks
Baby strollers, hard hats
Transit station alley cats
Humid Wednesday, rolls like a river
Before my south-side eyes

Cardboard Boxes by the Door

Home,
For awhile,
In my place
Packing a bowl, in my blue-lit
Living room

Boxes,
Empty
Sit by the door and leak nostalgia
They brought books to me in the mail
Books of poetry
Written by friends
Rum bums and
Mystic saints

Empty,
I used to fill boxes this size
With baseball cards, then
Postcards and love letters
Ticket stubs
From concerts and cinema
Boarding passes
When airline flights were rare events

All those paper
Souvenirs

Tan,
Cardboard boxes
No hope for re-use
I have little need for pulpy tabernacles

In this age
Of pipes and bottles and
Insomnia drenched
Texas nights

Gone,
Something has been lost
I do not even try to fill
The empty spaces
Begged by discarded cardboard boxes
Stacked up
By the door

Down to the Ocean in Hopes

She goes down to the ocean in hopes
Where tidal powers set hearts aglow
Like a full moon off a sand dune
The cycle renews itself

Quietly pulled to the liquid, unleashed
Free from expectations and experience
Universal flow is dancing

The streams and rivers that have scarred her life
Highways and streets, slashing through
Original wilderness, original paradise, original being
All return to where the sun surrenders to waves and depth

Poseidon and a million Sirens blow her hair
Into free-form tendrils
As she faces the maritime horizon

At the wet communion altar rail, she prostrates
With sand caking her knees and thighs
She petitions the ocean with a knowing smile
Her flesh exposed, like a tender bloom, too long in the desert

The elemental sacrament complete
She is quenched and restored
By the totality of Earth's nursery and vastness

This pilgrimage to the edge of other worlds
Has renewed passions for divine and vulgar things
With the fortitude of sub-Atlantic mountains
And the tenacity of threatened coral reefs

She has never been alone.

Distance

I do not have children
    nor
An alarm clock,
    nor
A newspaper subscription
I live consciously removed from the calendars of academia
Renting a house somewhere that is nowhere,
Remaining nonobservant of religious Holy days
    of
Cultural holidays;
Without even a television to section off my days
    into
News programs and talk shows

I find myself feeling alienated
Cast out of the marketing that defines modern lives
Things like "Back to School",
"Christmas",
"Football season",
"Rush hour",
"Tuesday"
All mean so little to me,
As I observe lives around me
Being bent and coerced
To the whims
    and
Demands of the collective.

Only celestial seasons to mark time
I measure my life, thus

South Texas, where seasons do not change…much
24/7, air conditioned, hermitage
    is
My lot for eight months a year,
Followed by those few, few weeks every orbit
When the climate is not trying to actively kill humans
    and
Other living things

I feel, sometimes, as if
I'm missing something,
Not having these demands
    or
Definitions forced upon me,
    and then I realize...
I am a paroled convict attempting to rationalize my way
     back into a cage...

It's called Freedom, man,
    and
If you can't handle it,
You really haven't earned it, yet...

I wouldn't trade this for anything,
Not even the melancholy that comes,
Not so much from missing anything, anyone
But from seeing so many,
Trade so much of themselves,
    away for
Such futile structure
Fleeting definition.

I am with the refugee,
The evacuee,
The alien...
The displaced and the marginalized
The broken
The beat

This is where my art comes from.
Distance is simply part
of
The destination.

10th Street

10th Street hangover morning
Contraband post office visit
Nuevo Progreso, Mexico
Yesterday

Pharmaceuticals and Cuban tobacco
Sent by mail, away
To a mountain state
In a cardboard box
Hair of the frog, soaking in
Blood Orange and Vodka
Edinburg in early December
Post election overcast
I only feel old
On mornings like this

I should have died decades ago
In aircraft wreckage and African smoke
What do the empowered young women see
When they look at me
Do they look at me?
Grey hair and a 38 inch waist
Leonard Cohen and Lana Del Rey
Coffee shops on mid-week days
Too close to call
Yet, too far away

Reflections are not reality
Ambitions do not defy gravity
But, those eyes
I want to drink her
Swim in her depths
As she reads James Baldwin out loud

Then,
She should leave me
With her taste on my face
For dinner with her fiancé

My knee never used to scream like this
My country never used to elect fascists
10th Street, all the way to Trenton
Past Ferguson, past Standing Rock
Past galactic check points
In time eternal
Curling back to someplace
Left behind for good
Past the prisons I refused to let control me

And what of youth?
And what of you?
And what of her?
And what of truth?

On 10th Street

Luna Lodge, 9119 Central Ave. NE

New Mexico

Quiet is a Color

Pull over at that Valero store in Boerne
 and fill up
Drop a tab and grab a bottle of cheap Shiraz
That'll get you to Fort Stockton or beyond
Don't worry about those
 highway lines
They never are as straight as they
 say they are

Greater vehicle, lesser vehicle
Cross-country psycho-star
West, until the burger joints
Start serving green chile
Meet me at the Dion's on Central
Up from all those beat motels
And I'll absolve you of all
 your travel sins
In the shadow of
 Sangre de Someone
Our Lady of Indulgence waits, tonight
Bag and kit in hand
 in glory land and blowing sands

San Antonio is not the place to be
If you want to catch a taste
Of the indigenous and wasted continent
Drive, you piece of shit, Drive!
Let those trucks slide by
Off your right side
Tripping circus light show Freedom chorus
Neal Cassady never washed completely away
Gorge your face with concrete, asphalt, flowers
Fuck it;

Destruction is your sole remaining comfort
Those thoughts and midnight relics
have grown fat and unresponsive
Always carry jumper cables on the highway
The lessons you get called to teach
may not be your own

The desert doesn't care this morning,
how long it takes you to reach Mountain Time
Zippo lighter on the floorboard
Always pick up hitchhikers
Tell Texans where to go
Happy oil-rig happenstance will guide their way

Quiet is a color, hidden in a knap-sack
Waiting on a fuel-injector blow job
Where did PeeWee Herman go?
Or Phil Niekro's knuckleballs?
Mad Swirl Dallas manufactured memories
Mistakes get made when you're stuck in 1988
You never thought those railroad tracks
ever really went anywhere
Finish the bottle, finish the throttle,
Ignore the whore
in Carlsbad
Run to Roswell, missing her
And all those sacred, down-home, oracles of time
Shut down desert Air Force bases
Where soaring things go to die

Quiet is a color, giggling on the fire escape
Signing on the boardwalk, hot dog,
line
Is not an admission of guilt

Failure to appear has been your life, I know
But now, you're really rolling
17 dirty dishes in the sink somewhere
    your slips and rips are showing
Like, when you were in the hospital in Big Spring
Ass-raping that god as you came to understand her
Restoring her insanity
(At least that's what she told me)

Every word in every book written
    along the Pecos and the Rio Grande, combined
Melt into your mouth, bleed into the sun
Like Townes Van Zandt
    strums "Highway Kind", tonight
Cross the floor to the Wurlitzer
Play "Nog" 'til Sunday morning
Nothing smells like government ink pens
Endorsing documents of doom and common sense
State-line gun show billboards
    stand topless
Money, death, and tears and birthday dreams
Tumble weeds are not, at all, erotic
So, ignore that hazy hard-on, when it swells
Recall the songs you sang in Sunday school
Reach inside your hat-band for that last joint
    rolled last night
Truth or Consequences on the exit signs
Yes, Jesus loves you, the Bible tells you so
Just don't ever stop the car
Don't ever take it slow

Quiet is a color on the dashboard
A relic you have never thought to seize
Someday these petroglyphs will matter

Someday even this heartless desert will care
I'll meet you at that pizza place on Central
If you ever make it all the way beyond

Quiet is a color at an orgy
It is Sandia Mountain sleeping pills
Tucumcari waits beyond tomorrow
Racing forms and Twitter lies combine
Coin-operated family planning clinics
On the walls of truck stop piss-rooms
Speak your name in wonder
Wonder where the fuel you're burning
    comes from
        Hum bums
Hum bum acid trips and cheap cologne
Swollen vulva mysteries of patience

Quiet is a color seen alone
That night they pinned that medal to your chest
And you stayed up drinking Bourbon
With the ministries of grateful, tie-dyed, death
The souls that paved the highway must have known it

Barista baritones are caged and singing
    of nebulas and brown dwarf stars, beyond
Pet Shop Boys and 1988 be damned
That train runs from Belen to Santa Fe
Locked up like Spanish priests in the Palace of the Governors
Quasars and calliopes burn the stake
White sage smoke fills your glove box
Paper cartons dance into the back seat on their own
Jehovah Witnesses knock upon your windshield
Thirsty for the wiper fluid blast
I'm waiting for you

Waiting here on Central
With working girls and run-a-ways and neon signs and drunks

I have a refugee eye and fingers that twitch
Ears that paint alibis when parole officers show up
Lies I have yet to share with dandelions blowing
Like Topo Chico boiling in the bottle
opened up at Louisiana Street bus stops

Be sure to stop at the Valero in Boerne
And top off all your tanks before you leave
The psychedelic highway waits and rises
Just beyond the limits of your rear-view

Quiet is a color seldom caught

Crossroads Motel, 1001 Central Ave. NE

Concessions

The sisters from the Pueblo come down to the river at dusk
Crosses hang from around their necks
Concessions to prevailing forces
    that come like the weather
Yet flow, like the waters
That rush off down to the
Rio Grande gorge

The flow rolls
Past indigenous red clay and brown skin,
And that stream shapes the landscape...for a season
Nourishing sage and ocotillo
From Taos mountain to el Golfo
The unquenchable things remain

Like the four directions, the four winds

Those missionary crosses shelter secrets
    in smoky, Tewa, tones

Angel Food

Don't believe that shit about
Angel Food cake and Ambrosia

In heaven they feed you Chick fil A
    every day
For eternity

Central and Eubank
(hurricanes and hand grenades)

Let's burn the Mayflower to her keel
On Central Avenue
Where the Caravan Club used to stand
Strafe la Nina y la Santa Maria
Messerschmitts and MiGs in tight formation
Rolling out over Cathedral Park
All that Contemporary Native art
    across the street

Let's confuse dreams with desperation,
    targets for destinations
The best choice off of a menu of shit
I'll take mine with raisins
My country 'tis of thee
    Land of inequity

This has been a season of hurricanes and earthquakes
The Earth wakes and tries to wash away
The sleep we keep slathering over her eyes
Fires burn and send smoke-signals down the range
Out, damn spot, Out!

Children held at the Falfurrias check point

Let us burn the Mayflower
Maybe, if we burned the Mayflower
Melted every statue of General Stonewall in the South
Maybe, if we cut the tongue out of ambition's mouth…

Who am I supposed to hate today?
Maybe the mirror, maybe the mirror

I don't have a mirror

Getting high with Rodrigo behind the closed down
Golden Corral
Across from the Conoco and Home Depot
Watching for cops

Contractors sweep the street
As that south wind
Blows Roswell sand up against
Solid stacks of Sangre mountains

Let's deny and ignore the Voyager probe
And dine on whale steaks tonight
By Jack Kerouac's yellow Roman candle light
Save a slice for Pizarro's ghost
Give Cabeza de Vaca head

Decapitate, decapitalize, and
Castrate the clerics
The shamans and poets, temple whores and troubadours
Outrage, drifting up
The Santa Fe trail

86 Route 66 and leave it to die beside
San Miguel Allende desert railroad tracks
Can't you see?
I'M BEATING HERE!

All the TV preachers in Texas couldn't fade
Your polyamorous polyglot experience
Cuban cigarettes and rumble seats
Albuquerque curiosity
Use those Allen Ginsberg books for kindling
    and burn the Mayflower

This blood-soaked hemisphere
Of so-called
    recent
        history

Close the borders
Evict the boarders
Close the borders
Now

Hang sheetrock where those
Shiprock closet doors should be
Can't you see?
We are re-modeling, here

7am substitute teacher phone call
Your brown eyes question
"What will the weather be like today?"
Hurricanes and hand grenades

Can't you see?
We're destroying idols, here!
Slicing heroes to bits
Praising inelegance
Tying virtue to rails of Mexican steel
Nobel prize TNT

Let it go to voice-mail
Let it go
17 times, already
Since she went away
    I've plunged that needle
        Into my vein
Here in the Mayflower's fiery glow

Inequity and ambition twisters
Like Mississippi step-sisters
No Trespassing signs and
    ammunition stashed
        behind the chapel door
Along with last weekend's newspapers
I have forgotten what I saved them for…

Burn the Mayflower on Central Avenue
Inhale the haze and wait
    grey and under-weigh
We should have never gotten used to having it
    our way
        every day

17 times since she went away

The price of the Ancients will never be paid

Hurricanes and hand grenades

Tewa Lodge, 5715 Central Ave. NE

Recovery

Recovery, Rehab
Court ordered counseling
Re-form what, exactly?
What if this is who I am?
All I'll ever be…

Recovery
Re-cover me
Cover me in conformity
Drug free
Banality

Sex and Smoke
Hate and Hope
Shooting dope
PnP
Easy lays
Hotel hook-ups and crazy days
Death oozing out of alleyways

Recover what?
All I ever did was die in Texas
Cover over who I am
With Serenity Prayers and treatment plans

I've been trying for decades to recover
That first blessed and worthwhile hit
And minimize risk from
Prison terms and OD deliveries
The machine gun fire is like
Seeing beyond

living the life
most would run from

Some of us choose to live on the edge
Before we ever consider going over
falling under

Riding thunder fireworks
And fucking demons
Makes us what we are
Arterial bleeding artillery
And other fleeting things

When mountain tops crumble
Who is there to understand,
How alive the thunder riders have been?

Do not tell me about recovery
Until that final freedom
comes for me

...Yet

That place you left
That place that you fled
That place that you wagered your hours,
    your sweat,
        your blood
To escape...

THAT'S where they will say
You are from
When you get to where you hoped to be
    against all hope
No matter what

No matter where you end up
A refugee is never welcomed
    never trusted
You will never know the steps to the dance
You cut in on
You are simply
Where you came from

We can flee all we can flee
But,
Do we ever truly
    get where we are going?
What refuge, what welcome
Lay in those golden, hoped for, lands?

Alone in a crowd,
New in the room,
    perpetually

With all of those eyes, greeting familiar others
  but not you,
    not yet

They are not inside jokes, traveler;

Their laughter just doesn't include you
  Yet…

Saturday Mornings
Artesia, New Mexico

Daddy's dark blue
Fire-proof
Coveralls
Oil stained
Steel-toed
Boots
Cigarette butts
Half-empty cans
Of Miller Lite beer
And Roustabout pay stubs
Litter the living room
Saturday Mornings

I'd sit, with cold cereal
And eat from the box
Watching fishing shows
On the television
Bill Dance, Jimmy Houston…
The tactics and strategies
Swam right past

I mostly remember
Admiring the scenery
Outdoors; on the water
And a boat that could go anywhere
Fish-finder sonar
That always knew, exactly
What lay beneath
Murky waters

It was always around noon
The voices would come from down

The plywood paneled hall
Words like “whore”, words like “work my ass off”
And “take that stupid bastard back to Texas with you”
And “cunt”

Daddy, all I ever wanted
Was a chance to get away
Get out
Get down
Down the highway, out of this desert
Out on the water
    On a boat
        That could go anywhere

Sailing for Friday night
    and knowing exactly
What to expect
    on Saturday mornings

Bow & Arrow Lodge, 8300 Central Ave. SE

Turquoise

My new
New Mexico
Lover
Reaches out, with the back of her hand
Presses into my shoulder
From across the divide of King sized comfort

And takes me for someone, somewhere, between
Willie Lomax and Walter Mitty
Fantasy and flesh in candle light and sage

"I will not cling to you, my lover"
Come her whispered, breathy words

"I only want to feel you
To touch you
For as long as you will share
This dark turquoise space
Before the dawn"

Righteous

Tale after tale
Like flood waters off a spill-way
He told her stories
One after the other
Like Dean Moriarty
But, more weed than speed
More chill than thrill
Maybe Neal Cassady's
  long, lost nephew
Raised a bastard
By Matthew McConaughey and Woody Harrelson

That old, Beat, espresso shop
At Vallejo and Grant
At Central and Amherst
At This and That Way
Taken for granted,
Like those San Francisco Franciscans, across the street
Take Eucharist

Talk about Texas
The North east Independent School District
  and small planes that didn't crash
And Charles Gatewood's photographs
Writers are natural liars
But, fiction has told more truth
  than text books
Black and white reveals kaleidoscope raindrops

He rolled on, the way the tide creeps in,
Up the Mississippi crescent
In New Orleans
Like George Jones, drinking, and riding lawn mowers

The espresso was fucking righteous
And so was she
And so was he…

Zia Motor Lodge, 4611 Central Ave. SE

The Road

West

This oil city sprawls below me
Orange sodium vapor lights
6AM departure
Friday begins

I'm leaving Texas for the San Francisco Bay
Bridges, words, and poetry await
A couple of mountain ranges away

Bath-warm Gulf waters in August
Do not cleanse
Pioneers soar these days
West, always west

Captain Whitman turns off
Our fuselage ID lights
Somewhere over the Sam Houston National Forest

West

High over two-a-day football towns
And marching band practice
Small cities in their entireties
Are concealed by the breadth and the chord of our aluminum wing

Boeing airliner roar is a whisper
Barely heard over highland lakes
Like Leaves of Grass to rattlesnakes

The Texas sunrise sky is clear this morning
Before 100 degree hate awakes
Boeing wings and poetry

Carry me

West

In Translation

She'd flick her ashes into
A Dr. Pepper can
Tell me she was
The survivor of a suicide pact
How she was raped, serving in the Navy
Jumped ship in Spain
And learned the language
Traveled for decades without visas
Fucking princes, painters, and heroin dealers

She took me to visit temples
Abandoned
Now that myth had overtaken religion
Happy Donut shops
Down the street from beat bookstores
Introduced me to men that knew men
That used to play piano in
North Beach Bars

That airport lounge in Dallas
Outfield seats to see The Dead at Wrigley
Day drinking martinis on Frenchman Street
For lack of a better plan

Her poetry stands up to the turning of pages
But she understood
That she'd always be
Best taken

In translation

Value Menu

Sometimes, I get too big for the world
My problems
Worries
Fears
Grow so large
That I must go out
Down the street

To the fast food shop

I will choose an item or two
Of some value menu, fried food
Just before noon
When the line is full
With hurried diners
On lunch breaks
From jobs they hate

"2 dollars and 98 cents, please"
The counter clerk will say
And I will riffle in my pocket
To produce quarters, dimes, and nickels,
Down to the last three pennies
Exact change is the only way this will work

It takes a while
So, I begin sharing
All about the troubles of my day
The fears I can exorcize no other way
Padding the tale with back-story
I mention peoples' names that no one here knows
The "I do not give a fuck" look on the worker's face
Is a god-send, as I lay coins on the counter

Line-standers behind me exhaling and shuffling feet
Impatiently, unwillingly, receiving my confession
Then, instantly, tossing it into the rubbage bins behind them

Perspective attained for less than three dollars
Less than 400 calories, if I order right
Less than two minutes…too long, really, for my fears and minor miseries
The fast food workers let me know
The line behind me, lets me know

And as I lay the last few coins on the counter
I smile at the refreshment
That comes from no longer
Carrying
All that
Loose change
Around

I walk away with a paper sack,
    full of reconciliation
My sacrament complete

2016 Literature and Latte Scrivener Award for Poetry, Hourglass Literary Magazine, Bosnia & Herzegovina

El Don Motel, 2222 Central Ave. SW

Just One Question

What did these brown, glass, bottles hold
These brass shell casings
These burned out homes

What kind of trees, where these ashes blow
These cavities, and missile silos

What kind of hole did these gods fill,
That used to reside in these once holy hills

What about these rusty syringes
Why were these tickets and schedules printed
Why were these iron tracks laid down
Why were these holes drilled into the ground

Who were these communiqués originally sent to
What good did these flags ever do

Why were these factories ever built,
And, why were so many, many, killed
How many meals were served on these plates
To those that were destined to quickly decay
Rusted cars and aeroplanes,
Where were they taking us, in the end

There must have been a struggle,
From the looks of things

What did these brown, glass, bottles hold?

Modesty

Boy-cut panties, crumpled on the floor
Weapons stashed behind the door
Crucifix bedroom-wall backdrop for
The sexting pic sent,
Un-asked

Modesty is a luxury
Hypocrisy
When life is exposed
For all to see

These are poems that never
Had a chance
Shot down, on some city street
At 25
By scared-to-death police
    still alive

Scarlet letters and prison terms
Credit scores and carpet-burns

Poetry bombed to bloody shreds
While waiting on friends
At a coffee shop
    that never came

Give your life away
Every chance you get

Like Allen Ginsberg's
Marijuana cigarettes
What you don't give away
    gets taken, anyway
Forsaken and destroyed

Poems picked up
Roaming the edges of freeways
With no tags
Cast away
Then, out of mercy
    gassed away

Like modesty, like secrets, like shame
What we give away
Comes back again

Like oceans turn to rain

Never Believe a Cop

Never, never, never
Believe a cop
Not a smiling cop,
Not an off duty cop,
Not a grieving cop,
Not a drunken cop,
Not a cop that looks like you,
Or that you grew up with...

Do not believe the things they say
When they use words like "War"
Or peace
Or justified
Or probable
Or cause

Never, never, never
Believe a cop

Because,
    you know,
They will never believe you.

Fly

Kick, Punch
Tear at the stucco and concrete walls
Destroy the stalls, just outside the gates
That promise clarity

I did not intentionally drown in this pit
I just opened my mouth
And the decay rushed in

1988 or 89
I can't remember, exactly, when
I was just a school boy then
Ripping and ranting

Beat

Beat the world, the sky
Beat the streets that hide
Molestations and homicides

Fly

Fly high, and higher still
On wings that Beat
Like poetry in alleys
Like a hustler at orientation
Like a root that's reaching for the sky

Like Lackland airbase boot camp
On a humid June night

James

She began to prefer taking tea, alone
In her SoHo bedroom
Often with the door to her tiny cell closed,
    heavy shades half-way drawn

Something about knowing that the neighbours' could
"See inside her pantry", she once tried to tell me

The unused airline tickets piled up on the bookcase,
Sent from New York City, round trip
By her sister
Invitations from the officially placed and decorated,
Along with Post Office phone bills
    unopened, unpaid

She'd only open her door for me
When I stopped in on Tuesday afternoons
And only if I promised to bring her news
Of how her son, James, who was killed in the Troubles,
Was making out, up in County Tyrone

She'd sit, and talk, those afternoons
As I picked up a bit,
But she'd tell me it was time to leave
As shadows darkened her slow, sad, room

"Fine, just fine," I'd always tell her,
"He can not wait to get back home
Should be back, any day, now."
She'd smile and walk me to the door
"That's why I just can't travel, these days
I need to be here, for my James."

Then she'd lock the door behind me

And I'd head to Millroy's on Greek
To wash down my dishonesty
With the slightest shine of her ancient eyes
as I do every week

Hiway House Motel, 3200 Central Ave. SE

Out of Control

Completely
Out of
Control

We should all be there
So that we learn the way back

So that
We learn
That there is
A way back

Before the court,
Guilty,
In chains,
Waiting to hear
How long
They will lock us away

Shot and bleeding
On a dirty street

Trapped inside
Burning wreckage

Knowing that
Prayers will not
Make rescue
Any more swift
Or certain

Powerless to stop

The aftershocks
Or to still the winds
Or to turn back
Flood waters

Or falling bombs

We should all be there
So that we learn the way back

So that
We learn
That there is
A way back

So that
We learn
Not everyone
Makes it back

Complete

Friday the 13th
(Paris 2015)

Gunfire in nightclubs
And bombs in foreign cities
Do not lead me to poetry

Instead, I will uncork
A bottle of Abouriou

Perhaps; later,
If I can find the spoon
If I can find the sugar
I will pour some Absinthe

And watch
The louche
Paint Van Gogh
Swirls

Of not quite peace
Yet, not quite war

Denver Poem

Cassady's red brick
Denver downtown
Across from that
16th Street bookstore

Chesty the bulldog and I
Sit;
Waiting for Jack's Beat Cowboys
In this ocean of hip

Trains and buses and garbage trucks;
The ancient street sweeper,
Work,
Move,
    and Dance the Cosmic tango of the day

As we; for a while
Just sit
And stay
A thousand miles away
From home

I Took Another Mind-Ride Last Night

Black room dark with mirrors where I stood
With suddenly Asian features
Younger, full cheeked and erstwhile
I changed into a beautiful woman
Then a grotesque one, then an aboriginal child
Smiling

I saw myself from inside of the husk
Worn by a dying Nordic beast
Adrenal overload threw me to the ground
And I crawled closer to the mirror
Mirror with no edge or end
Placed my eye directly on the glass
I was seated on a bed in early winter

The full and solemn peace of high ordeal, satisfied
Came to me
The drug high of The Fear
That raged before was gone
I knew that somewhere near
An erotic cabaret was playing
I heard Ella Fitzgerald reading the poetry of Katie Hoerth
Kittens, lapping milk, could be sensed
Along with the barnyard calliope of commuter trains
Shrimp were being served on the flight deck

Axial tilt realizations
It was Girl Scout cookie season

"You don't have to be here when you die"
The voices told me in conspiracy
"Some of us haven't checked back in for years."

21 Motel, 2411 Central Ave. NW

The Holiness of Hayward

Refuge is a shadow
7 Eleven at
Jackson and Sycamore
Hayward, California
Black hooded bodhisattvas
Sit in a circle beside the dumpster
And take communion from brown, paper, sacks

Cool, August, East Bay night
Brings refuge
I know and I do not know
The deep-traveled joy
These monks have earned
In shadows

Hiding from
Well lit, antiseptic
Policing powers,
Scavenging saints
In black hooded sweatshirts

Treasures lurk in places
We have learned not to look
Jackson Street rubbage bin zendo.

Stratosphere Hotel

I nuzzle your neck
And move lower

You press against and pull me down
Hand tangled in my hair
To taste
The thickened nectars from last night's lovers

Prayer vigils
Do not stop
Mass Shootings

The waters of Babylon
  Make steam
    From fires of Eros
      And imagination
You are the aroma of honeysuckle and salt air
Enjoyed by honeybee and hermit crab, alike

Never tarnished or abased by their attentions

Metal detectors
Do not stop
Hate

Words and hopes and wishes
Do not stop
Bomber jets and battle tanks

…and in the morning
    you fill my nostrils and mouth
Like a sunrise, poured into
A Las Vegas hotel room

Love
For all its rapture
Does not end pain

Desert dwelling paramours
Do not build walls around such oases

Palms die when they do not learn to sway and swing
And negotiate
Multiple realities of need

It does not stop
It does not stop
It never ends

Shores of the Cannon Ball
(Mni Wiconi)

Encamped on the banks of the Cannon Ball
It's about more than the water
But, it's about the water, first
Mni Wiconi

Those glaring lights, in a line
Across the Cannonball River
Hide brown shirted deputies
And armed vigilantes
They wait without irony
Intent, on vengeance for Custer
Peace officers and citizen-soldiers
Their language is on their side
While journalists ignore....when they do not lie

All day and night
The engines drone, above
Peering down, like vultures
Drones of prey
Marking time, marking us all
The high water mark of hope,
Amid these river-worn stones
Monitored through rifle scopes

Black snake, oil tar-sands
Dollar bills and corporate clowns
Beat us back and mow us down
A winter flood is coming
Shielded in blue
Cyber attacks from voting booths
Rolling in, with armor
What they cannot tame, they come to conquer

Elders and medicine women dance tonight
Water protectors in small fire lights
Sing songs that never ended
Across the Cannon Ball
Mni Wiconi

It's about so much more than the water
But, it's about the water first
Mni Wiconi

De Anza Motor Lodge, 4301 Central Ave. NE

If I Die in Philadelphia

If I die in Philadelphia
Let it be somewhere Beat
Somewhere like the Penrose
Down by that Christmas light factory
If I die in San Antonio
Let it be in an alley
On the Southside
Somewhere off of Rigsby Avenue

I want to live until my last breath
Walking beside Cerrillos Road
A glass pipe in my pocket
I want to shout into the desert night
Somewhere south of Tucson
Praising the Marfa lights

Let me stow away on a C-17
With soldiers heading home
Let me listen to their stories of youth and truth
Let me wander off to Jupiter
Then catch the Sunday red-eye back
Let me swim in a tumbler of Bourbon
Somewhere a little north of Little Rock

Let my body lie in state
With William Burroughs
And Emiliano Zapata
At the Echo Hotel
Room 508
Or in a Copper Canyon hostel
In early spring

And, the day after I die
Let me lurk in your red lit room
Let me taste the fire in your eyes
As he takes you time and time again
Marigny Bywater lust
Setting the zydeco afternoon aflame

Unchained

This is Not SLAM Poetry

This is NOT SLAM poetry
My way is the page
And the page is a stage

The truth is the way
The word springs from the page
And the lights and the crowd
Too loud to allow
The subtleties of mind
To rewind and find
That the spirit of the poem

Flows beyond the rhyme
Beyond the poet
Beyond this night
After the fight
After the might
Far beyond the bite of our second sight's
FLIGHT

My stage is the page
My glory and doom
Sitting, alone in your room
On a stand by your bed
Silently waiting for you to open it up
Silently shouting, bound and collected

The page is my stage
The stage manager is you
No cheers or applause
Can make truth more true
This is NOT a SLAM poem
As I read from the page

‘Cause my mind, it will fail
It will wither away
Slither away
Memories will lie
And the sun will rise
After every night’s dream
We’ll open our eyes
Vanities burn bright
Beneath our disguise
And I’ve been living too long
To expect any damned prize

Except for the page
The page will survive

The page is my stage

This is not a SLAM poem

Shambhala Stupa

Hidden, white, shining
Stupa
Basic human goodness
Celebrated
Amid the pines
Wild flowers, bees, and mountain breezes

Sing mantras to those that will listen

A path to mindfulness
Through halcyon, elevated, ether

Closer to God…
    perhaps…

Closer to the self that is not ourselves

And has always been

Weather Hold
(airplane mode)

Stuck
On an east coast taxiway
Two hours
Then three
Away from the gate

Weather hold by air traffic control
Control the air space
But never the atmosphere

Crumpled into a window seat
I practice the patience of tectonic plates
On a Sunday night
Southwest flight
Full of families- children cry
Demanding movement- like earthquakes

And I've set my patience and acceptance

To airplane mode

San Francisco Postcards

I want to mail you San Francisco postcards

Postmarked Philadelphia, PA

I want to lay with you in Dallas

Curtains open,

Neon skyline glowing on your skin

I want to find you waiting there

At baggage claim

In lingerie,

Damp thighs and hungry eyes

I want to fuck you from behind in Denver

In some beat joint on Colfax

And grab and squeeze your neck

As your Corpus Christi climax

Washes over us

I want to sit with you in dimming light

On a porch that faces south

And speak candidly, with humor

Of lovers we have found

Taken, made, or used

Let us celebrate the carnal,

With coffee

And consecrate what's true

San Francisco postcards last forever

The postmarks never do

Spirals

I dig the perspective of poets

Elder professors and

Age addled -Heads

Beats that somehow survived

The scars of their lives

And sit now

To write

In public places

Since empty nest homes

Have become too lonely

Those that know it is an endurance race

On a circular track

Perhaps a spiral

Perhaps downward

Grey eyebrows furrowed

Above eyes that have never

Stopped searching the horizon

For a sunset or sunrise of beauty

I dig those with no more answers

That can easily see past

The next November election

That can love without

Wagering their own Identity

(Dedicated to Dr. Chuck Taylor, Jr., PhD and Dr. Harold Rodinsky, PhD)

Special preview from PW Covington's upcoming collection of short fiction:,

North Beach

I sprang from the back of the car in front of the North Beach Hotel on Kearny, my legs uneasy.

I'd made it halfway across the country on five cocktails and two commercial airliners, landing at SFO about an hour after the early November sun had run off the edge of the continent. The regal, worn, Asian woman at the counter had me sign what I needed to sign..."No smoking in the room", "No guests after 10", yeah, yeah. She made a copy of my ID, the Texas driver's license with the very dated and very menacing, shaved head, Fu Manchu 'stache, just-out-of-prison-long-enough-to-grow-the-damned-thing, picture. I got the code to the Wifi and took the elevator to my room, 116...on the third floor.

The hallways were dark....old, but clean, carpet in forest green checks, and dark, varnished wood. The place was a shit hole, but it hadn't gone to shit through dereliction or neglect. I knew that a lot of effort was being put into keeping this shit hole the kind of shit hole that it was.

Glorious North Beach shit hole. Perfect shit hole. Non-gentrified, proletariat, shit hole. One of the last. Bodhisattva shit hole, hallowed be thy name.

I unpacked my single case in a flurry. Enticing smells wafted up to and through the opened, unscreened, window in my room. A mix of Chinese noodles, Korean BBQ, something sweet like doughy jelly...man, I was fucking starving. I'd eaten at Gatti's Pizza before leaving Austin and had hoped that would be enough to see me through until morning, but the drinks and the sudden energy of the vibe of the people of the street of The City got to me.

I needed to eat something.

There was a hunger that wouldn't be denied. Maybe there was a diner around.

Back down the elevator, out the front door, past the regal, worn, mistress of all things that needed signing, I turned to the right.

The noodle places, both of them, that I had taken note of whilst spinning out of the car earlier were closing up, so I keep walking until I came to a corner.

I never go into a place when they are closing, I try to respect everyone enough to give them a chance to knock off from work a minute or two early. Back to families, lovers, loyal dogs and hungry house cats. The signs here were mostly bilingual, written in Chinese and English, some only in Chinese, but a noodle shop is a noodle shop no matter how it's advertised, right? And every fucking one of them was closing up for the night.

The street climbed, uphill, and pulled me along, past neon red kissed awnings, Jackson Street daring me into Chinatown proper, but no...not tonight, not right now.

Food.

The smells of restaurants, all five minutes from closing, kept luring me, fueling my feet, my mind left out of it, mostly. This was pure Id. An alley opened up and loomed on my right, just past a place called Bund Shanghai... red paper lanterns hanging from a third or fourth story balcony.

These two seconds, I knew I'd remember forever in the heart of my mind's eye.

Yes. Yes. Loving it.

But, no to Chinatown. Hungrier now, and walking faster...there has to be something still open. Another right on Beckett, narrow, holy Beckett Street, with its murals and clothes hung out to dry on balconies. Neon buzz drifting on the cool, moist, air. And, that's where I headed...following the red and yellow glow up Pacific to Columbus. The pit of my stomach was growling.

A smoke shop, glass pipes and bongs in the window. I walk into the deep space. Glass counter tops and two men in the very back. I need some screens.

I brought my pipe along in my checked bag, and just enough stash not to be detected. But, the screen's been needing changing for a while, clogged with the resin of a hundred sleep-starved Texas nights.

The dark-eyed olive men look like brothers, thin, stubbled beard faced, and eager. All I need is some screens.

How many you want, the tallest brother asks.

How much do you charge? (back in Texas, the shops sell them 10 for a dollar).

I can sell you a whole bunch for like 5 dollars, the guy says.

I don't need a whole bunch; I'd just lose them. Just a few will do.

The shorter, darker brother laughs. Yes, I know what you mean.

Tell you what, how many will this get me? I fish out 2 one dollar bills from my pocket and lay them on the counter.

The clerk puts 10 dime sized screens into one of those tiny plastic bags that you only see in the drug culture. This one has tiny pink mushrooms printed on it.

I thank them both and leave the head-shop grotto, back out onto Columbus, right past Vesuvio. The ghost of angry, bitter, fat, drunk, glorious, Kerouac taunts. We have drank together here before, on previous visits, but won't tonight.

I walk past tourist couples from the Mid-west taking photos in the alley. Digital cameras and cell phones. No more negative images; everything is perfect, everything is instant, everything existing as a mirror image and shared. Proof we are here, proof we were there, but no proof of life. Close though, and some days, some trips, close is good enough.

It's close enough for the workers at City Lights; glowing, cathedral, fluorescent, bookstore. They are sweeping the floor and tending the shelves.

This is the heart so many times broken.

The hunger in my stomach, like the hunger of that sidewalk...Tosca taunts from across the street.

A busker with a massive white dog beside him on the sidewalk, probably the real thing, probably a rail rider, a hitch hiker, a pilgrim...he's tuning his guitar, but never actually playing it. Looks sober, too sober for this night and I nod to him as I walk by. The nod says, I've been there before, maybe I still am, never give up on yourself, brother, you can fuck life in the ass all night long and still respect it in the morning. Live, pilgrim, live...but I know that he knows all this.

There, right there, right after Ferlinghetti's best idea, at the right place and the right time, I find it; a little pizza shop, serving by the slice.

I only need one. Pepperoni.

Nothing tastes like hot, street pizza. Texans never get this right.

The cat at the counter, ethnic, gives me a slice on a thin paper plate and it is so hot it burns my hand as I hold it.

I leave the shop and lean up against the wall outside, the corner of Broadway and Columbus, looking up the street at the gaudy, tantalizing, moving neon promising topless dancers and cocktails. The Condor, Roaring 20's, Big Al's, and the Beat Museum.

It's enough for me to just stand here, the pepperoni of the universe folded in my hands, orange-red grease staining the white paper plate. I stuff it into my mouth like a man who has a bus to catch and an alibi to conjure.

The older man, black with his road-worn cotton beard, standing next to me, wants me to buy his newspaper, and I just can't. He understands, and we talk. We talk about cheap food in Chinatown and strippers and whores. He claims he can get me a girl, but I know what he really wants is a 5 dollar bill. I change the subject to the weather, at least it's not raining, as 10pm tourists flow by, all between bites of the best pizza, the sought after and found pizza, the Beat pizza right next City Lights, the neon born and west coast pizza, street style Italian.

About a million times better than Mr. Gatti's Austin. It's not just my stomach I am feeding.

Spanish, Chinese, German, the word-sounds from passersby tell me that this is international pizza, that mine is international hunger, that the man beside me is internationally Beat. From this street corner, where Muni busses and fire trucks turn; to the farthest, darkest, star; galactic hunger, it's all that anything's ever been, right here.

Not much more to it, really, just that Galactic Beatness.

It still exists...even here, where it is packaged and sold; so, I finish the crust and fold the plate in half, then in half again, then in half again. Grease stained wedge.

I turn away from the cotton bearded man, who seems to be heading across Broadway somewhere, off towards the twin spires of Peter and Paul. I float back by the beautiful busker and his wonderful white dog, tossing the oily plate wedge into a street-side trash can.

Like the hotel, this street is seedy, worn; but clean, respected, maintained.

Beat is being down, but not out...never out... never out of the game, never out of chances, never out of hope, never out of style.

Back past the glass windows of City Lights...books on display like holy Mexican santos statues. The sacred only works when it's approachable.

How many have sat upstairs with the poetry, not as shoppers, or even readers....but just to sit and listen to the walls, the shelves, the roof top laundry drying just outside the open windows? How many have rushed in, just to buy a T-shirt or bumper sticker, to take a Facebook photo or... ?

Columbus runs at a diagonal, crossing both north-south and east-west streets, all the way through North Beach, and I follow it now, back onto Kearny, back towards the hotel.

There is a sink in my room, but I haven't a cup or glass, so I duck into a boba place and grab a large green tea with black pearl boba. The young clerk makes it right in front of me, as I drop my change and a dollar bill into the tip container. I grab the tea and a straw and walk back out onto the street. I'll drink it when I get back to the room.

Into the lobby, past the regal woman who seems to be turning things over to a pudgy male clerk...The elevator is full of twenty something Korean tourists, hip-hop ear buds and hooded sweatshirts.

“3”, I say, when one of the young women asks me, switching to English for my benefit...the old white guy, probably down on his luck...probably lives in this shit hole...be kind to him, he’s a big guy, but harmless, her dark eyes say, as she presses the button.

Look for “North Beach and Other Stories” by PW Covington, in 2018

Special thanks to Edward Vidaurre and Alan Oak, who graciously reviewed and offered notes on this collection as it was being prepared for publication.

Photo by Leslie A Jensen

Thank you so much for taking the time to read these poems of mine!

Consider leaving a review on Amazon or Goodreads.

Since the release of "Sacred Wounds" by Slough Press in 2015, the support and encouragement of readers like you has been humbling and wonderful!

We are living in a golden age of Indie publishing, and current events, for better and worse, keep us all in steady supply of material.

Keep Living! Keep Resisting! Keep Writing!

-PW Covington, ABQ NM, Nov 2017

Follow PW Covington on Instagram and Twitter @BeatPW

Follow the author on Facebook and contact him at
www.PWCovington.com

PW Covington is represented by Authors, Large and Small
For booking and media inquires, please Email:

Cristina Deptula
cedeptula@sbcglobal.net

95082606R00068

Made in the USA
Columbia, SC
06 May 2018